The Wordsmith's fragments

BALSHREE PIYAIBALA AYAM

BookLeaf Publishing

India | USA | UK

Presentation by *BookLeaf Publishing*

Web: www.bookleafpub.com

E-mail: info@bookleafpub.com

ISBN: 9789363315846

First edition 2024

To my beautiful daughter, Kiyana...

ACKNOWLEDGEMENT

I extend my heartfelt gratitude to all those who have contributed to the creation of "The Wordsmith's fragments," enriching the pages with their wisdom, support, and inspiration.

To my husband, for his unwavering love and encouragement and for being the bedrock upon which I stand.

To my daughter Kiyana, who is the happiness bounty of my life.

To Tamcha for everything.

To Dr Rashmi Sharma, for the constant nudge and encouragement. Your wisdom has shaped me into the writer that I am today.

To Dr Indrani Chowdhury and Dr Madhu Pant, for their patience and guidance.

To Anushree Kulkarni, for being the most kind and empathetic proofreader.

To the readers, for your openness and willingness to embark on this literary adventure with me.

And finally, to the muses – the seemingly muffled voices of inspiration that have guided my pen and infused these pages with meaning.

With deepest appreciation,
Piyai

PREFACE

In the delicate medley of life, there are moments that shimmer like dewdrops on a petal and others that weigh heavy as stones in the riverbed. "The Wordsmith's fragments" is a collection of poems that seeks to capture the essence of these moments – the fleeting joys, the enduring sorrows, and the quiet resilience that binds them all.

As a woman, daughter, mother, and corporate employee, I have traversed the diverse landscapes of experience, each fragment leaving an indelible mark on my being. In this collection, I urge you to journey alongside me as we explore the complicated threads of womanhood, family, and career, weaving them into a rich story of emotions and reflections.

Through poetry, I have endeavored to distill the essence of these experiences into words to be read and lived. Each poem is a window into a moment, a memory, a revelation, and more crafted with care and imbued with the depth of lived experience.

In "The Wordsmith's fragments," you will find echoes of laughter and tears, whispers of love and loss, and the quiet strength that buds from the human spirit. I hope that these poems serve as companions on your own journeys, offering solace, inspiration, and perhaps a glimpse of the beauty that lies within the fragments of our lives.

With gratitude,
Piyai (Balshree Piyaibala Ayam)

Untold

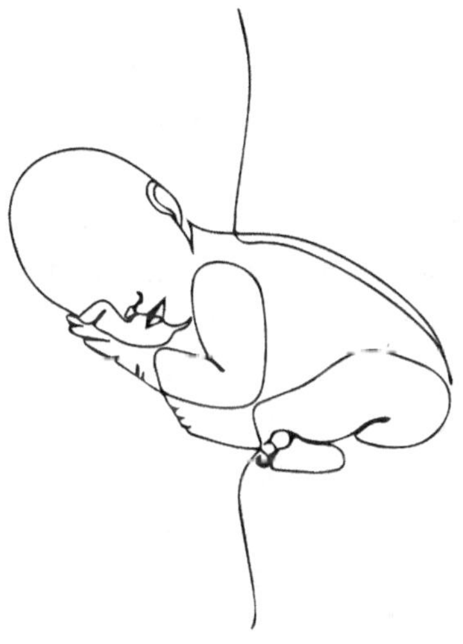

In the womb's sacred sanctuary, a bud awaits.
A silent promise, sealed by fate's cruel hands.
A promise. A trust.
Wrapped in the tender embrace of a mother's
sighs.
Like a delicate flower, she's meant to unfurl,
But destiny is twisted, her future tainted.

Her petals, like dreams, remain tightly wound.
As shadows of fear cast darkness around.
Like a pearl in the shell, she's a treasure unseen.
A vision of beauty, a future pristine.
She's the whisper of hope in a world so bleak,
But her existence fades, on a caprice.

The shadows lurk.
She flickers and fades.

Her essence, a symphony of potential untold,
Yet the hands of despair snatch her from the
fold.
Like a bud plucked from its stem too soon,
Her presence fades beneath the soothing moon.
The painting remained unfinished.

In the garden of life, where dreams take flight,
She's a bud denied the sun's healing rays.
Her fragrance, lost in the winds of desolation, in
the night's silent despair,
Just as a tragedy is woven into society's loom.

Mourn for them.
Buds torn from the vine, destined to wither.
For daughters lost. For their universe untold.

I am that woman

In the whirlwind dance of modern life's fray,
She strides with grace, not a minute but through
the day.
With a child's hands clinging to her and dreams
in sight,
She anchors the realms of livelihood.

In fierce boardrooms, she stands tall and bold,
Weaving a story of wisdom and strength.
Yet, when the day's battles have all been won,
Her nurturing heart is never done,
Helping shape her daughter's wings,
She someday, too, would dare and fly high.

The bedtime tales are no less a task than
balancing deadlines.
For she conquers mountains, leaving inspiring
trails.

A resilience forged in the fires of time,
She conquers trials, subtle and prime.
With burdens heavy and paths unclear,
She treads with resolve, ousting fear,
In the shadowed alley of society's gaze.
Her days are a tapestry woven with care,
Balancing bills, worries, and a mother's prayer.

She is a beacon of might.
She guides her child through the darkest of
night.
In her love, her child finds grace.
However turbulent be life's relentless race.

She is the melody.
She is the rhythm.
She is the song that is sung.
I am that woman.

Depth

A moment ago,
It was about the height that I wondered.
This very moment,
It's the depth I am surprised at.

In the quiet depths, where shadows reign,
And silence holds a lingering sway.
I find myself in the night's embrace,
Where stars whisper secrets,
A secret of forgotten chance.

I dive into the abyss, where time stands still,
And confront the echoes of my own will.
Gazing.
I see the rippling past, the mystery…
A moment ago, I sought the height.
But now, in the depths, I find my light.

Like a phoenix rising from the ashes of
uncertainty,
I emerge from the depths,
Breaking free from the dearth.
For in the depths,
I find the courage to soar,
And grip the depths I once abhorred.

Submerged in the depths of introspection,
I find solace in unravelling mysteries mile by
mile.
For it is in the chasm, where truth lies,
That I find the answers to my whys.

In the depths where the shadows roam,
Freely and wilfully,
I find the courage to call this place home.
Each step forward, a leap of faith,
Owning the depths, unafraid of the wraith.
For it is in the depths, where I discover the
height,

Of the strength to carry on.
To break free from my shell.

The Office Odyssey

In the land of ties and polished shoes,
Where power games are never to lose,
Lies the realm of corporate lore,
Where office politics thrive and soar.
Yet, in the cubicles, beneath the fluorescent sky,
The clock ticks slow, and the coffee goes cold.

Behold the executive chamber, a battleground
grand,
Where suits and egos clash, so much for a status
quo.
With smiles as fake as plastic veneers,
They plot and scheme in clandestine chants.
A cruel charade.
The captain of the ship, a king upon his throne,
Rules with iron fists, cold as stone.
His minions scurry, eager to please,
While stabbing backs with practiced ease.

In meetings long, they play their parts,
With empty words and rehearsed arts.
The elevator pitch, ever so perfect.

The jargon flows like a murky stream,
As they chase elusive dreams.
The breakroom, a battlefield of gossip,
Rumours fly like arrows, cutting through verity.

Promotions dangle like a carrot on a stick,
But only for those who play the slick.
But each climbs a ladder, each rung a breach.
A twisted game, a puppeteer's illusion.
Pull the strings. (Do I see the sinister grin?)
They preach diversity and inclusion,
What ethics? What morals? Flamed.

Laugh at the folly, the absurdity,
Of corporate life and pomposity.
Let the Odyssey end.
Find your peace, just around the bend.

Silent Noise

In the tumult of the mind, where conflicts brew,
The silent noise ricochets, a tempest's hue.
It whispers of doubts, fears, and desires,
An opus of mayhem, as the soul aspires.

In the labyrinth of memory's maze,
The noise nudges in mysterious ways.
And snakes through the corridors of time,
Past and prime, subtle and sublime.
In the depth of contemplation's well,
The silent noise resounds a constant swell.
It murmurs of choices, both right and wrong,
A strain of discord, as convictions throng.

In the silence of indecision's clasp,
The silent noise hums, relentless.
In the layers of consciousness, where thoughts
collide,
The silent noise mutters, unable to hide.
It drifts through the currents of hope and fear,
A harmonious blend of anguish and tear.

Hold on.
The noise is silent.
As it speaks of forgotten celebrations.
In the quiet corner of the mind's recess,
There's the swarm of laughter, once bright and
gay.
Like a distant breeze, passing by.
A chorus of wistfulness.
The heart's thrall lies cherished.
The noise – silent as ever.

Migraine

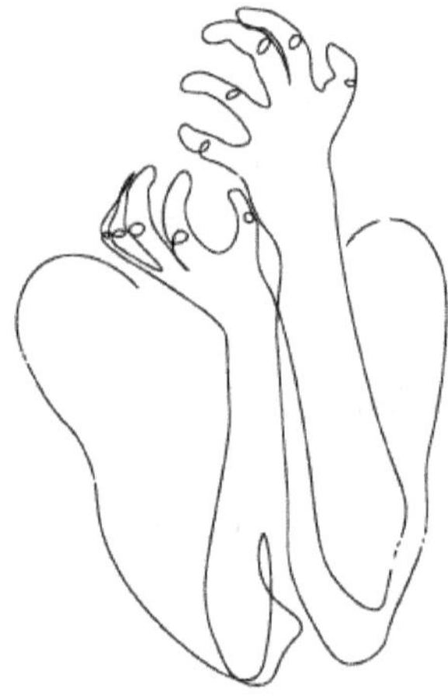

Thump… … thump… Thump, thump, thump…
Begins the cruel dance of migraine's somber
tone.
Softly at first, ever so slightly across the corners
of the eyes.
A subtle wail.
Then the gale of a crescendo forces into being,
Fierce and frail.

Its tendrils reach, ensnare the mind and the soul,
In its grasp, lucidity is vacuumed.
Each pulse, a hammer striking deep within,
As agony takes a sinister spin.

Thoughts are plagued.
Excruciated by the pain.
Vision baffles the sight, spirits tested and tried
for.
Reasons struggle to maintain its foothold,
Tossed adrift by waves of suffering.
Searing the very fabric of consciousness,
Migraine's fury wields its punishing scorn.

Throb, throb, throbbing…
Where throbbings entwine,
Naxdom and Vasograin emerge, divine.
Their names chanted like prayers,
In the battle against the migraine's plight.
A shield of relief.
Until the next episode.

No, I couldn't write

Words once danced.
Today, I sit with thoughts entranced.
But inspiration, maliciously elusive,
Leaves my pages untouched, very elusive.

I search for a glimmer of light,
But my thoughts remain cloaked in the night.
The once-familiar rhythm, now lost in the void.
Leaves me stranded, feeling like a paranoid.

I reach for words, but they slip through my
grasp,
Like oblivions fleeing from a tightening clasp.
My mind is a barren land.
Creativity fails to take a stand.

Slivers of muses, distant and faint,
Mock my futile plaint.
For in the stillness where words should thrive,
There's emptiness, hard to revive.

Yet in this silence, a seed may sow,
A spark of inspiration, though slow.
For every drought, a rain must fall,
When shall new verses call?

I linger in this void.
For I believe, new dreams will be buoyed.
And when the muse returns, with the dawn,
My pen will dance, reborn.

Cancer

Of a mother's muffled suffering, I write.
Her pain concealed behind a smile so bright,
Each whispered ache, a burden borne alone,
In silence, she suffered, her strength unknown.
Cancer gnawed her in solitude.

Through days of struggle, she never let on,
Her love, her shield, her light, now gone.
Her gentle whispers, mistaken for complaints,
By her children, malignant, distant.
Cancer gnawed her in solitude.

But oh, the depths of her silent plea,
Ringing now, in memory's decree.
For in her quiet misery, she bore,
A mother's love steadfast to the core.
But cancer gnawed her in solitude.

Words unuttered, her love was clear,
In every sacrifice, in every tear.
And though she's gone, her spirit lives on,
In the hearts of her children, forever drawn.
Cancer gnaws them.

Her absence gnaws.
Isn't it huge, grief's claws?
Though parted from the earthly shore,
Her love remains, forevermore.
Cancer gnaws.

Fragments of peace

In the heart of Manipur, where nine mountains
rise,
And valleys stretch beneath azure skies,
I reminisce about days long past,
When beauty and peace were to forever last.

In the embrace of verdant hills,
Life felt at home.
Your rich culture, luxuriously benevolent,
Welcomed each. Loved all.

Oh, Manipur, in your glory, you stood,
A land of promise.
Your mountains, majestic, kissed by dawn,
Your valleys pristine, a tranquil lawn.

Times changed. The contention of strife,
Have shattered the serenity of life.
Ethnic clashes slit your soul,
Leaving scars that time alone cannot heal.

The fire scorched the ties of brotherhood,
And raped the bond of humanity.
Of homes that were burnt, I write.
And honour that was raped.

The rivers that vein through,
Is no longer a stream that quenches thirst.
The river's course through the land,
Oh! but in the colour red.

The forests that once teemed with life,
Dies barren. Brazened.
Impudent knives cut through the lives,
Scattering dark corpses. Raped.

Yet amidst the chaos, hope still gleams,
In the enduring dreams,
For the spirit of Manipur, strong and true,
Shall rise. Peace shall renew.

Oh! Remember the beauty of yore,
Heal. Unite once more.
For in unity lies Manipur's might,
To reclaim the glory, to shine bright.

Starved

Hunger stirs.
Starved of hope,
What can chase away the endless night?

Hunger slanders.
Starved of dreams,
What can click the chains away?

Hunger gnarls.
The screams silenced.
What can revive the withered dreams?

Hunger clutches.
The being crumbles.
What can ignite the flickering flame?

Hope dwindles fast.
The heart leadens.
Defy the hunger.

Rise.

Raped

Concrete.
Too solid that it hurts.
Thoughts that scrubbed away humanity,
Leaving scars unseen but deeply felt.

It's a maze of Gray.
Anguish seeps.
A soul suffocates.
Each breath trapped,
As darkness engulfs, with no one to care.

In the hollows of the wounded soul,
Where pain dwells,
A heart once bright and cheerful,
Now closed and cold.

Each scratch haunts.
Each tear rips.
The sands shift.
The ground beneath twirls.

The soul battered refuses to wane.
The wounded spirit,
Aches to break free,
Flutters to reclaim life.

Each memory a dagger, a piercing cavern,
Each moment a battle.
The soul is bruised of honour and trust.
The cries fractured.

The hurt's sting burns afresh.
The stained skin gives away the sear.
Is there a mend?
Does it ever heal?

The scrapbook

I peek into the scrapbook of life.
Pages unfold.
Each moment captured a story untold.
Memories stitched perfect patches of time.
A weave of laughter, of tears, of rhyme.

The first page announces a baby's first cry.
A mother's embrace.
And a proud father's declaration.
Tiny footprints sprinkled across the page.
A voyage of love, ready to commence.

Through childhood's joys and adolescent woes,
The pages gain pace.
Schoolyard friendships, secrets shared in trust,

Kindles of love, juvenile in accent.
A kaleidoscope of remembrances.

Chapters of trials follow suit.
Heartbreak and loss.
Love that would otherwise cement hearts.
Dim hours and prevailing hope.
Yet guiding the way through stormy gales.

Love's cloying embrace,
Binds and interlaces two hearts.
A wedding vowed and promises sealed.
Etched in love.
Hand holds hand, life takes the turn.

The pages yellow.
As the years pass by,
Dreams fulfilled, or dreams shattered,
In the scrapbook called life,
Every page is willed, there's no turning back.

The final pages may be Gray,
Look almost grim.
The last pages are the ultimate.
A legacy bright,
A testament to a life lived.

Mosaic of small delights

The memories of small things,
The not-so-big ones,
Are so profound in life.

Those before-dawn walks,
With Pabung always ahead of me,
Those first pink streaks of the sun's morning
glory,
The dews glistening on the grass blades,
The lax smell of the untended.
Yes, they are significant.

The ritualised morning cup of green tea,
Those little exhilarations
As Eema's toasted bread wafted through the
house,
Tingled my olfactory senses.

The rustle of pages turning,
I lost myself in the worlds within,
The comfort of a familiar story,
A refuge from the din.

The laughter shared over meals,
The jokes and banter that never fail,
In those simple moments, life reveals,
Its beauty, its depth, its tale.

The sound of rain on windowpanes,
The pitter-patter of drops through the ceiling,
Brings consolation, brings peace,
As worries and troubles gently cease.

The stars that twinkled in the night,
A celestial dance, a mesmerising sight,
In those moments, big or small,
We find the essence of it all.
For life's true splendor lies within,
The nuances of where we've been.

*Pabung– what I used to call my father
*Eema– Mother in Manipuri

Quest

In the depths of the mind,
Tangled and enormous,
Where thoughts swirl,
Like leaves in a wintry flare.
The sun of clarity seems overcast.
The confused mind rambles,
Lost in the contrast.

Through mazes of doubt,
And shades of fear,
The path ahead is unclear.
The sun obscured by clouds austere.
Confusion reigns.

The bewildered mind,
Though storms may rage,
Within voids, a wisdom sage.
Embrace the journey,
Turn the page.
For clarity awaits,
Beyond the cage.

A spiderweb.
Snarled and muddled.
Each thought intrusive.
Each decision, a question.
A dissonant tune.
The voice is cacophonous.
The confused mind,
Searches for a room.

Shrouded in plea,
The sun decides to shine.
There is a silver lining.
The mind finds a way,
Triumphant, desolate, and free.

Quenched

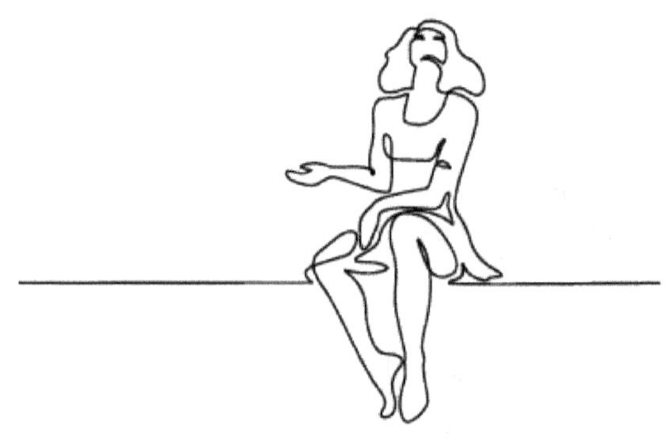

The unforgiving glare,
Sunbeams scorch the arid air.
She wanders weary and bare,
Weary of trials,
Bare of tribulations.
Thirsty lips are parched,
Her senses trick her.

The sands she treads on.
The sands of time mock her.
Each footstep, heavier than lead,
Heavy with responsibilities.
Her throat a desert, her soul in dread,
Seeking comfort, a drop to be fed.

Shimmering mirages fail her,
Illusions abound.

Hope flickers, then falters,
Nowhere found.
Yet in the distance, a sight of promise.
A glistening oasis.
Hope.

With trembling hands,
And a mutter of gratitude,
She drinks the elixir.
Dreams are born.
Tides. Waves. A gentle breeze.
The peace that she sought.
Conquered.

She finds her place.
The haven of her own stride.
Grace and pride become her.
The chase, as if it never was, extolls.
Her dreams make her whole.
Courage. Beauty.
There no longer is the thirst.
Quenched.

Aged

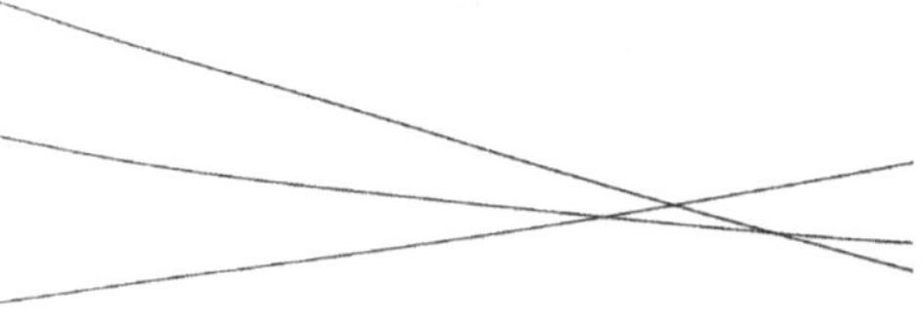

The past has concealed itself in oblivion.
There's no trace of evidence.
Of those bracketed smiles
Or of those freelanced emotions.

When again, I saunter.
By the eucalyptus-lined streets.
My senses are mingled.
With the same, used-to,
Rustic beams of morning sun.

My perceptions, I realise,
In the same old, unforgettable way,
Are undoubtedly intercepted,
By the unaltered tranquil perfume
Of the still wet morning mist,
The damp earth.

Are they suggesting something?
Are they proving the absence,
Of such a thing
As change on this earth?
Or of the stagnant meaning of life?

Yet, the early sun
When it bathes the porches gold,
Or as it casts shadows,
On the street by the eucalyptus,
As it warms the window frames.
In everything.
There seems to be,
A very punctual hint.
A vague, undefinable understanding.
Momentous.
It lingers; I can feel.

Oh! It grows very distinct now.
A frightful confirmation.
Of age.

They told me of their own age and mine.
Humming together, the tune of life.

Pitch and toss

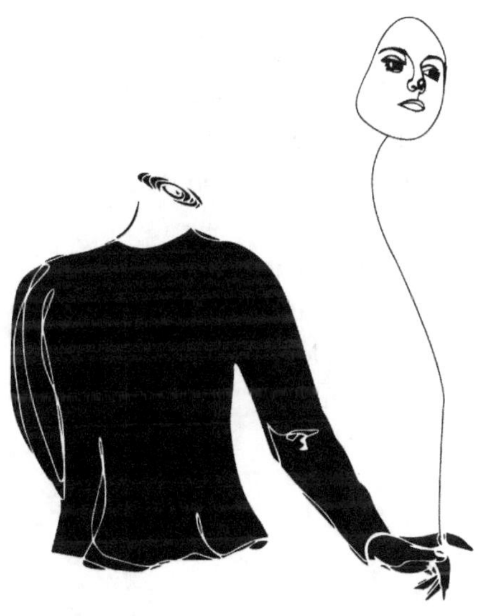

Life's a pitch and toss. We sway.
Like ships on a tumultuous bay.
Through high and low,
We ebb and flow.

With every toss, a chance to rise.
To seize the moment, reach for the skies.
Yet in the pitch, we stumble.
We fall. We crumble.

Each pitch, an opulence.
Stormy seas and tranquil shores dance.

Up and down, twists and turns.
Groove. Challenge churns.

Life's a game of chance and fate.
Victory and defeat often mate.
Toss, we find our new strength,
To anchorage the bout at length.

Each toss a lesson, each pitch a test.
Embrace. Answer the quest.
In its folds, joys gleam.
In life's grand scheme.

Silhouette

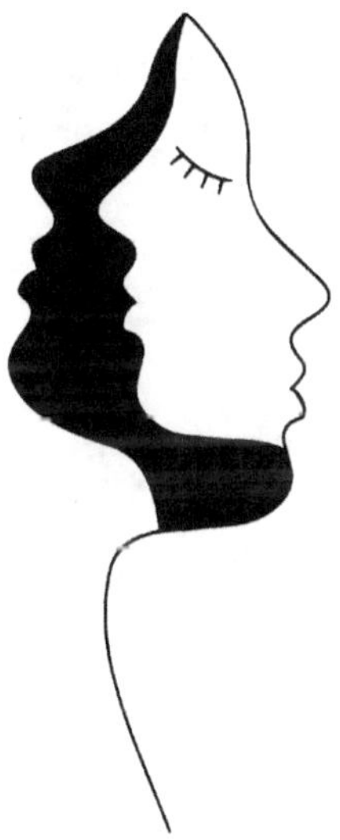

Amidst the darker hues, a tale unfolds,
Of secrets kept and stories untold.
Of obscurities, where light grows dim,
Lies the silhouette of life's transient whim.

Fleeting.

A dance upon the sky,
Murmuring verses of a world gone awry.
The silhouette seems monstrous.
Its expanse preposterous.

Outrageous.

Dreams collide.
And the darker shades confide.
Beneath the cloak of dusk, sorrows dwell.
Yet shards of hope prevail.

Anticipate.

The silent strength emerges.
With thousand urges.
Shadows sprawl.
The monsters crawl.

Unyielding.

Appraisal, the farce

The appraisal's farce, a scripted show.
Is it politics? Or is it bias?
Symbiotic, they grow.
In the dance of ratings and rankings,
Fairness and transparency thwart.

A charade of judgement, truth can't quell.
Behind the metrics, we meet.
A theatre of numbers, a stage of pretence.
With forms to fill and boxes to tick,
Merit and performance toss over.

In the spotlight's glare,
The employee's trial prolongs.
Trials of worth reduced to numbers.
Weak are the cases.
The shallow scheme wins.

No disguise pacifies the hurt.
No author changes the narrative's course.
For years of spectacle,

The rigid frame triumphs.
Malevolent.

Elided

A stretch of a curve around my eyes,
An inch in length,
Usually extra on my lips,
This was me as I knew myself.

Sleepless nights.
Insomniac days.

A wrinkle of pain around my eyes,
A line of strain in my forehead,
An arc of stress across my brows.
Certainly, this is not the 'me' I knew.

As seasons pass and time unfolds,
Each mark, a story waiting to be told.
In every furrow, there's wisdom,
In every wrinkle, a lesson retained.

But in the mirror's gaze, I find,
Reflections of battles, the grind.
Each line, each crease, a tale to tell,
Of struggles. Of hurdles. The scar.

I embrace each line, each trace.
Each is etched with courage.
A testament to resilience, uncouth.
Yet an unmistakable reminder
Of strength within, rife.

Ceremoniously

It was a grand affair; all for her family, uncles,
aunts, and nieces.

Amidst ethnical differences, ethical objections,
subjections, and suppressed grudges,

Their seemingly wistful union took place; for
them it was all love. Ceremoniously.

They were spectacularly and very much in love;
they flew with the wings of dove.

My fair-skinned, handsome sister-in-law married
my meek, professional brother.

Oh! There has been a slip; my brother was
married to her.

My sister-in-law was accepted into the
household, properly, customarily, willingly.
Welcome.

With her entrance, many stabbing immaterials
and comforting materials entered our home.
Welcome.

Shining furniture, dazzling modern gadgets,
sophistication, and a good amount of undecided
zeal,

To the bedazzled neighbours and inquisitive
visitors, she marked her exquisite appeal.

To herself, she was generous, proud of her
'used-to' extravagance, and very satisfied.

Very young and a bit untampered, she took pride
in her contemporary, unorthodox ideology.
Glorified.

An uncompromisable status quo, my
sister-in-law had inculcated in her, her maiden
name.

An equally strong status quo, my family had
nurtured in her of her, however, little fame.

My father tethered us with strong values. He was
a father in every sense– strong willed and poor.

With an aura of unsatisfied intelligence, he was
kind, impartial, educated, religious, and very
poor.

With his resourcefulness and unending
diligence, he took our concern; never did he
throw up his cards.

As offsprings of his traits, besides every
deprivation, every year each of us received
report cards.

"Your material ends will be met with once your
intellectual ends are met with," my father
believed.

My brother lived up to his expectations,
academically, got himself a profession. My
father was proud; relieved.

Unexpressed, but in his old heart, there was
love. He loved us; he needed to be loved and
cared for.

He loved the society equally, worked for the
cause, unbiased and sincere. This he was
respected for.

The cause broke the thread of my mother's
affections. My sister-in-law called it pretence.

My brother, as fate would have it, turned out a
true husband. My dear old father's pain was no
pretence.

My mother was lovely, with an irritable-at-times
degree of endurance, very much a mother.

She couldn't learn much of books but everything
a hard life teaches, very caring as every mother.

Unceasing work had hardened her hands, but her
touch still balmed our household, my dear
mother.

She has sincerely welcomed my sister-in-law,
anticipated her to be her friend, a dear daughter.

My sister-in-law, while very decidedly, was very
much a daughter-in-law in every way by law.

Her absence was always accessible during the
family's thick and thin, ups and downs, highs
and lows.

My sister-in-law, uneased by our family's
economic porosity, hunted out in our persons
uncurable blisters.

She couldn't miss out on them– the whispered
tete-a-tete, gossip that plunged into the family
through her sisters.

Fate must have had the same prophecy. Each
family of our genre with such societal tint
always had it.

Clashes had to be there. The lion of the
condemned destiny sprung out roaring. The fire
of doom already lit.

My sister-in-law unwound herself from the grim
family ties; my brother chose to be her husband
undoubtedly.

Our battered home witnessed another ceremony.
A farewell, the snapping off of a family, not
traditionally.

Serial Whisperer

Shadows tower
And secrets cower.

A whisper stirs within my mind,
A voice so soft yet so unkind.
A conscience, both a guide and foe,
In whispered tones, its truths bestow.

It speaks of dreams I dared to chase,
Of choices made, and moments' grace.
Yet often, too, it questions why,
And leaves me yearning for a reply.

The night is still. Dead. It calls,
A whisper from within the walls,
A voice that threads through every thought,
By conscience wrought, by struggle caught.
The serial whisperer, quiet, deep,
In concealed corners, secrets keep,
It murmurs truths I dare not face,
Reflects my flaws, my fall from grace.

It speaks of paths I am yet to tread,
Of words unspoken, tears unshed,
It questions choices, lost, and found,
In silent echoes, all around.

For every whisper, there's a heaving plea,
Find the better me!
To every nudging thought, it lends its blend,
A force that bids my soul relent.

Through battles waged in silent night,
I seek the dawn, the morning light,
Introspection, hard and true,
In whispers old and whispers new.

A dialogue self-begun,
Under the gaze of a setting sun.
In this struggle, raw and steel,
I touch the depths of what I feel.

A search for peace, for inner calm,
To quiet the whispers' pressing qualm.
For in the core of every sigh,
Lies the reason why I try.

The serial whisperer, ever near.
My conscience clear, my truth sincere,
In whispered tones, it leads the way,
Through night to dawn, to light of day.

Mind's rampart

Mind.
Silent walls.
Guarded thoughts rise.
And Brick by brick,
Beyond doubt, doubts build towers.
Fears settle like dust .in nooks.
All Dreams press against the iron gate.
Hope still flickers, casting warm light on stone.
Through cracks, courage dares to seep. The heart
pounds.
A force to breach, the rampart crumbles. Those
silent walls.

Redundant

A maze of thoughts that twists and shouts,
Redundant fears start to creep about.

They wear old shoes with soles worn thin,
Repetitive whispers of joy and pain.

Hope rises, falls, and rises once more,
A night's flare with the same old clout.

Desire stirs with predictable beat,
A heart that races, then admits defeat.

And sadness—ah, that familiar face,
It drifts through rooms with haunting grace.

The wilted bloom,
But always leaves without a trace.

So here we are, a loop in time,
Dancing to rhythms that never rhyme.

These fortressed emotions, so profound,
Are just echoes in a merry-go-round.

But in the end, what do we find?
That these redundancies, so unkind.

These are the threads that stitch us to the ground,
Binding us closer than ever before.

Through my fingers

Resolve.
A decision weighed, yet swift,
In the shadows of your desires,
Our love began to drift.

Your need for control, a bitter barb,
In the garden of our bliss,
I watched darkness wrap,
Each gentle, tender kiss.

You craved the edge of sorrow's blade,
A dance with aching fire,
I, lost in tender reverie,
Fell victim to your pyre.

With every tear and whispered plea,
Your pleasure found its mark,
Yet in the echoes of your glee,
I stumbled in the dark.

I loved you with a fervent strain,
But couldn't bear the cost,
Each night you found delight in pain,
A piece of us was lost.

So, I let you slip through my fingers,

Of love that flourished in the light,
Untainted by the grief,
I sought a world of simple flight,
A haven of relief.

In the quiet aftermath,
With echoes soft and clear,
I hope you find your path,
Without the shades of fear.

For as I let you slip away, a chapter's end in
sight,
I hold on to the hope that dawn will bring me
gentle light.

9 789363 315846